NATURE ANATOMY
GUIDED JOURNAL
FOR KIDS

65 Prompts to Spark Adventure and Explore the Natural World

KRISTINE BROWN, RH (AHG)

ILLUSTRATIONS BY KIM MALEK

ROCKRIDGE PRESS

First Rockridge Press trade paperback edition 2022

Rockridge Press and the Rockridge Press logo are trademarks or registered trademarks of Callisto Media Inc. and/or its affiliates in the United States and other countries and may not be used without written permission.

For general information on our other products and services, please contact our Customer Care Department within the United States at (866) 744-2665, or outside the United States at (510) 253-0500.

Paperback ISBN: 978-1-68539-270-3

Manufactured in the United States of America

Series Designer: Jane Archer and Karmen Lizzul
Interior and Cover Designer: Richard Tapp
Art Producer: Sue Bischofberger
Editor: Laura Apperson
Production Editor: Cassie Gitkin
Production Manager: Lanore Coloprisco

Illustration © Kim Malek
Author photo courtesy of Andrew Dobson

10 9 8 7 6 5 4 3 2 1 0

CONTENTS

Your Nature Anatomy Journal iv

YOUR NATURE ANATOMY JOURNAL

Welcome to *Nature Anatomy Guided Journal for Kids*! Keeping a nature journal is a fun way to track everything you learn about the natural world.

My name is Kristine Brown, and I'm a homeschooling mom and nature lover. Over the years, my kids and I have spent lots of time outdoors exploring the woods, fields, and streams in our area. My kids enjoy journaling about their nature observations, so I'm excited for you to use this journal during your own adventures. The questions included in each section will help you ponder nature, and you can write your own personal reflections and observations in the blank spaces as you explore.

This journal works well with my book *Nature Anatomy Activities for Kids: Fun, Hands-On Learning*, though it can also be used on its own.

Continue reading for a brief summary of the topics covered in this journal, as well as tips on how to think like an explorer and act like a scientist.

OBSERVING THE NATURAL WORLD

This journal is broken down into five themed sections related to our natural world: the sky above us; the planet Earth and the earth beneath our feet; the water all around us; the different types of plants; and the critters that roam Earth.

THE BIG BLUE SKY

This section is all about what happens in the sky, including the weather and clouds, the sun and moon, and the stars that fill our night sky.

WEATHER AND CLOUDS

Weather is a natural event that brings us sunny, rainy, windy, hot, and cold days; snow; lightning; hurricanes; tornadoes; thunderstorms; and tsunamis.

Clouds are closely related to weather. When water evaporates from the earth into the air, it clings to dust particles, which form the clouds. Heavy clouds full of water form precipitation.

Weather patterns that repeat in an area over a long period of time are called climate. An example of climate is the existence of seasons: showers in the spring, heat in the summer, more showers in the fall, and snow in the winter.

EQUINOXES, SOLSTICES, AND SEASONS

Earth orbits around the sun while rotating on its axis. It takes Earth 24 hours to complete one full rotation, which is why one day is 24 hours. Throughout the year, Earth's tilt and orbit around the sun

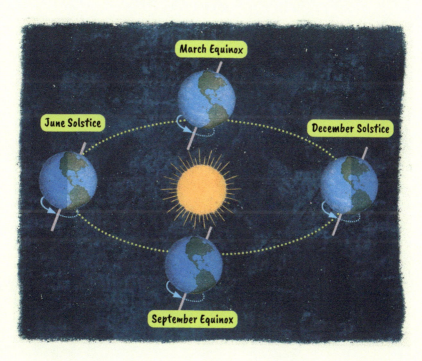

March Equinox

June Solstice

December Solstice

September Equinox

Equinoxes, Solstices, and Seasons, cont

bring us closer to the sun and farther away from it. This causes the sun to appear in different parts of the sky and for different lengths of time throughout the day, which gives us equinoxes and solstices. During the equinoxes in March and September, Earth's tilt causes an equal length of day and night. The summer solstice, the longest day of the year, happens in June, and the winter solstice, the shortest day of the year, happens in December. These equinoxes and solstices also mark the change of the seasons.

THE MOON'S CYCLE

Over a period of 27.3 days, the moon orbits around Earth, creating eight phases. In addition, the moon makes one complete rotation on its axis in 27 days. The moon's surface reflects the light of the sun. As the moon orbits, sometimes it's between the sun and Earth. Other times, Earth is between the moon and the sun. We cannot see the sun's reflection on the moon when the moon is between the sun and Earth.

This positioning creates the new moon, which is completely dark. When Earth is between the moon and the sun, we can see all of the moon, creating a full moon.

The moon grows larger, or waxes, from the dark new moon to the bright full moon. After the full moon, the moon becomes thinner, or wanes, so it looks less full during this time. It takes almost 14 days to go between these two phases.

STARGAZING AND CONSTELLATIONS

Stars, like our sun, are made up of hydrogen and helium gases that form a hot ball with a core of nuclear fusion. Stars are in groupings, called constellations. Ancient people used to imagine connecting the dots of constellations to create images such as animals, sea monsters, or mythological people. Just like we see the sun in different positions throughout the year, constellations are also seen in different locations in the night sky throughout the year. For example, in the Northern Hemisphere, Orion can only be seen in the fall and winter.

Ursa Minor
The Little Dipper

THE GROUND BENEATH US

This section covers everything about Earth, including its rotation, revolution, and structure; its rocks and minerals; and its landforms and landscapes.

EARTH'S ROTATION AND REVOLUTION

Earth spins, or rotates, around its axis in a counterclockwise motion. The axis is an imaginary line that runs from the north pole to the south pole through Earth's center.

Earth's Rotation and Revolution, cont.

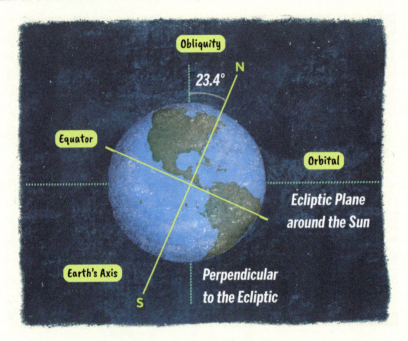

The axis is tilted at an angle, called the axial tilt. Earth takes 24 hours to complete one rotation on its axis. As Earth's rotation faces us toward the sun, we experience day. When Earth's rotation faces us away from the sun, we experience night. Because Earth moves counterclockwise, the sun appears to rise in the east and set in the west.

Earth also rotates around the sun as it spins on its axis, which is called a revolution. This takes 365.25 days, creating our calendar year.

EARTH'S STRUCTURE

Our Earth is made up of four layers. The innermost layer is the inner core, which is a solid sphere made up of iron, nickel, gold, silver, platinum, palladium, and tungsten. The next layer is the outer core, which is a liquid iron layer. The inner core spins much faster than Earth, and it creates Earth's magnetic field. The third layer is known as the mantle, which is divided into the lower and upper mantle. The lower mantle is mostly solid, while the upper mantle is semi-molten to solid.

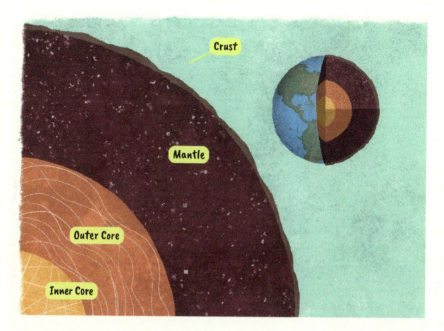

The final outer layer of Earth is the crust, which is mostly made up of silica and aluminum. There are two different crusts: the continental—or land—crust covers 40 percent of Earth, and the oceanic crust covers 60 percent of Earth.

ROCKS AND MINERALS

Igneous   Sedimentary   Metamorphic

Earth's crust contains many types of rocks and minerals. Minerals are made of one or more chemicals. There are lots of different classes of minerals, including carbonates, oxides, silicates, and sulfides. Some examples of minerals include salt, quartz, silver, copper, magnetite, and calcite.

Rocks and Minerals, cont.

Rocks are made from two or more minerals clumped together. They can be hard or soft, and there are three kinds: igneous, sedimentary, and metamorphic. Rock examples include granite (igneous); limestone and coal (sedimentary); and marble, quartzite, and slate (metamorphic). Rocks and minerals are used in many different common household items, from paint to computers.

LANDFORMS AND LANDSCAPES

Earth is made up of many different landforms, which are naturally made features such as mountains, hills, volcanoes, and canyons. These landforms, along with other natural features and plants, create our landscapes, which are all the visible features of the land that surrounds us. An example of a natural landscape is a desert, whereas a city skyline is a type of human-made landscape.

THE WATER THAT SURROUNDS US

Learn about the types of water that can be found on Earth and the ecosystems that live in them.

BODIES OF WATER

Bodies of water, like bays, bogs, creeks, rivers, lakes, and oceans, can be filled with salt water or fresh water or a combination of both. Bodies of water are important to all living beings on Earth. They supply passage around the world, drinking water, rainwater, and habitats for creatures that live in water.

SALT WATER VS. FRESH WATER

The two main types of water on Earth are salt water and fresh water. Salt water contains a large amount of salt, whereas fresh water contains a small amount that is not noticeable. Another difference between the two is their densities, or weights. Salt water is heavier than fresh water due to the amount of salt it contains. When a river or other freshwater system flows into a saltwater body such as an ocean, the two types of water mix, creating brackish water, which is less salty than salt water but saltier than fresh water.

SALTWATER AND FRESHWATER ECOSYSTEMS

Bodies of water contain a community in which living organisms interact with nonliving factors to create an environment that supports life. This is known as an ecosystem. Saltwater ecosystems, or marine ecosystems, contain three main zones: the splash zone, the intertidal zone (which contains both the high-tide and the mid-tide zones), and the low-tide zone. Freshwater ecosystems contain three community groups that keep them healthy: producers, consumers, and decomposers.

THE PLANTS IN BETWEEN

This section invites you to explore the plants on Earth.

DIFFERENT TYPES OF TREES

White Ash Leaves   Horse Chestnut Leaves   White Oak Leaf

Eastern Pine Needles   Douglas Fir Needles   Cottonwood Leaf

Different Types of Trees, cont.

There are more than 60,000 different species of trees. All trees can be categorized as deciduous (often called broadleaf) or conifer (often called evergreen). Deciduous trees lose their leaves at the end of their growing season, usually autumn, then resprout their leaves at the beginning of the next growing season, usually spring. Deciduous trees use their leaves to collect sunlight, rainwater, and air to help the tree make food. Conifer trees are cone-bearing trees. Their leaves are needle-like or scale-like and their shape prevents water loss, so they hold on to their leaves year-round.

PLANT POLLINATION

The Anatomy of a
WILDFLOWER

Petal · Stigma · Style · Anther · Stamen · Filament · Pistil · Ovule · Sepal · Ovary

Most plants reproduce through a process called pollination. Their flowers contain reproductive parts, and they can be pollinated by either wind or insects. Pollination happens when the wind blows pollen from one plant to the female reproductive parts of another plant or when insects such as bees, butterflies, and wasps carry pollen on their bodies from plant to plant as they drink nectar.

THE CREATURES IN BETWEEN

There are many types of creatures that roam Earth, including birds, insects, and animals.

BIRDS

There are between 10,000 and 13,000 different species of birds in the world. The most common types of birds in the world are songbirds, birds of prey, and waterbirds. Songbirds, like robins, nightingales, and warblers, are the birds you most commonly find in your neighborhood, and they have a song box, called a syrinx, that allows them to sing. Birds of prey (also called raptors), like vultures and hawks, hunt smaller birds and other animals. Waterbirds, like ducks, geese, seagulls, and pelicans, live on or around water.

INSECTS

An insect has three body parts—a head, a thorax, and an abdomen— three sets of legs, and one or two pairs of wings. You might be familiar with some insects that live in your backyard, such as bees, butter- flies, crickets, grasshoppers, and ants. Although insects may annoy or scare you, they play an important role in the environment. Some help pollinate plants, some keep pest insects in check by eating them, and others help clean up by feasting on dead plants and animals. There are between 2 million and 30 million different types of insects, and scientists say that there are more than 10 quintillion (10,000,000,000,000,000,000) insects roaming Earth at any given time.

Insects, cont.

The Anatomy of a
DRAGONFLY

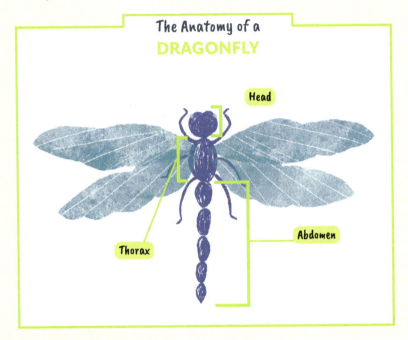

Head

Thorax

Abdomen

NEIGHBORHOOD ANIMALS

The Anatomy of a
SKUNK

Mostly black fur with white striping from back of head to tip of tail

Black and White Bushy Tail

Ear

Eye

Nose

Sensory Whiskers

Each foot has five toes and claws

Back Paw Print

Front Paw Print

Not all wild animals live in wild places. Because there are so many people on Earth, animals have learned to adapt and live among us. Some animals you may see around your neighborhood include raccoons, skunks, squirrels, deer, foxes, and coyotes. Some of these animals, like raccoons, skunks, foxes, and coyotes, are nocturnal, preferring to sleep during the day and be active at night.

EXPLORE AND RECORD LIKE A SCIENTIST

Use your nature journal to explore, record, and illustrate the world around you like a scientist.

EXPLORE, RECORD, AND ILLUSTRATE

Start by **exploring**. Be sure to do the following:

1. Start locally, in your backyard or a local park. You'll be surprised at what you'll find!

2. Carry everything you need in a backpack.

3. Bring specimen containers and bags to collect items.

To **record** what you find, follow these tips:

1. Bring along this journal, a pencil, an eraser, a fine-tip pen, colored pencils, a magnifying glass, and a ruler to make recording easy.

2. Find a comfortable place to sit while you write.

3. Give yourself plenty of time to observe before you begin recording, and pause often to continue observing.

Once you've explored and recorded, try **illustrating**.

1. Start out illustrating with a pencil. Once you are satisfied with your drawing, you can go over it with a fine-tip pen. You can also color your drawing with colored pencils.

Explore, Record, and Illustrate, cont.

2. Make labels for the object you are drawing, including the size of the object and any characteristics.

3. Label your illustration with the location, time of day, and weather.

FOLLOW THE SCIENTIFIC METHOD

Scientists and explorers follow the scientific method whenever they want to learn more about nature. Here are five simple steps that you can use to learn more about the natural world.

1. Observe: Look over the situation or object that you are studying.

2. Ask many questions.

3. Use your imagination to answer the questions that you have from observing your environment.

4. Test your answered questions to prove yourself right or wrong.

5. Reflect on all the work that you've done.

STAY SAFE!

Finally, follow these important safety tips.

1. When working with plants, never eat anything, no matter how tasty it looks. Always use caution when touching unknown plants, and be sure to wash your hands afterward, especially before touching your face.

2. When observing animals, make sure you stay a safe distance from them and do not get in their pathway. Animals become defensive if they feel threatened or cornered. Consult with your local wildlife guidebook or conservation officer for specific safety guidelines regarding the animals in your area.

3. Don't go into a body of water without a proper flotation device and/or without a grown-up nearby.

4. Be mindful when observing inclement weather and do so only from a safe location.

Can you think of any other safety measures you should take when exploring the natural world?

HOW TO USE THIS BOOK

Use this journal in any way you want, wherever you want. Fill it out from start to finish, or randomly pick a topic that interests you. This journal is not dated, so you can work through it at your own pace. You might wish to write a date on the page as you go through a section so that you can look back and see when you started learning about something. At the end of each section, you'll find a space for freewriting. Use this space to record your observations, questions, and illustrations.

If you find a topic particularly interesting, use it as a starting point to explore more about that topic on your own. Great explorers keep learning and exploring.

This journal can be used as a companion to *Nature Anatomy Activities for Kids*, but it is not necessary to have that book to use this journal.

I'm so excited that you've chosen to be an explorer of the natural world. There are many amazing things to discover, and I know you're going to have a blast. So, turn the page and start exploring!

Cirrocumulus

Cirrostratus

Cirrus

Altostratus

Altocumulus

Stratocumulus

Cumulonimbus

Cumulus

Stratus

Nimbostratus

THE BIG BLUE SKY

When you go outside and look up, what do you see? During the day you may see the sun, clouds, and sometimes the moon. At night, your sky may be filled with stars and the moon. In this section, you will journal all about the sky and the things that fill it. Are you curious and excited to learn about the sky? Let's get started!

DID YOU KNOW that where you're located geographically determines the type of weather and seasons you'll experience? What does the climate look like where you live? What does it feel like?

TAKE A DEEP BREATH of fresh air. Did you know that even though we can't see air, it still has weight? Why do you think air has weight?

HAVE YOU EVER SEEN fog rise from the ground? What do you think creates fog? Do you think fog is the same thing as a cloud? What makes it different from a cloud?

THERE ARE 10 different types of clouds in the sky (see page xviii). Can you name them and sketch their shapes? Where are they located in the sky? Hint: Some are high in the sky, while others are near Earth.

DID YOU KNOW that you can tell what time it is by the position of the sun in the sky? Why do you think this is? Can you think of any ways in which ancient people used the sun to mark time?

A SUNDIAL IS A WAY TO MARK TIME based on the shadows cast by the sun at different times of day. Ancient civilizations used sundials to keep track of the hours of the day. How important do you think marking time was to ancient people? Why?

WHY DO YOU THINK many cultures built stone circles, such as England's prehistoric stone circle called Stonehenge, which marks the solstices and equinoxes?

OBSERVE THE MOON at night for several days in a row. Does the moon rise at the same time every night?

IS THE MOON the same size every night? If not, why do you think the size changes?

_____
_____
_____
_____
_____
_____
_____
_____
_____
_____
_____
_____
_____
_____
_____
_____
_____
_____
_____
_____
_____

THE MOON CAN BE SEEN in eight different phases as it orbits Earth. What is your favorite phase of the moon and why?

A SOLAR ECLIPSE happens when the moon moves between the sun and Earth, temporarily blocking out the sun from our view. What do you think happens when there is a lunar eclipse?

DO YOU EVER go out at night and look at the stars? Why do you think stargazing was so popular in ancient civilizations?

DO YOU KNOW any of the constellations in the sky? What are some of your favorite constellations and why?

_____

_____

_____

_____

_____

_____

_____

_____

_____

_____

_____

_____

_____

_____

_____

_____

_____

_____

_____

_____

_____

HOW DO THE CONSTELLATIONS in the Southern Hemisphere differ from the ones in the Northern Hemisphere?

OBSERVATIONS:

_____

_____

_____

QUESTIONS:

_____

_____

NOTES AND SKETCHES:

OBSERVATIONS:

_____

_____

_____

QUESTIONS:

_____

_____

_____

NOTES AND SKETCHES:

Hematite

Clay

Mica

Halite

Magnetite

Chalcopyrite

2

THE GROUND BENEATH US

In this section, we are going to turn our attention to the ground beneath our feet! What is Earth made of? What types of landforms are around you? What makes up a landscape? What can we do with the rocks and minerals that Earth is made from? Are you ready to explore how cool Earth is? Plant your feet on the ground and start observing!

EARTH IS ALWAYS SPINNING—or rotating—in a counterclockwise motion. That's why the sun appears to rise and set each day. In the morning, where does the sun first appear in the sky? Why are there different time zones all around the world?

IT TAKES EARTH 365.25 days to make one complete revolution around the sun. What would happen if we didn't add an extra day to our calendar every four years?

_____

_____

_____

_____

_____

_____

_____

_____

_____

_____

_____

_____

_____

_____

_____

EARTH HAS FOUR MAIN LAYERS, which include the inner core, outer core, mantle, and crust. Why do you think it's impossible to dig through all the layers of Earth?

ALTHOUGH EXPLORERS HAVE been able to map out most of the continents by physically exploring the continental crust, the greatest depths of the oceanic crust have not been so easy to explore. How do you think scientists are helping explorers learn about the shape of the oceanic crust?

DO YOU KNOW the names of any rocks and minerals? How many can you name? Which rocks or minerals are your favorites? Why?

THERE ARE THREE different types of rocks. Can you name them? How is each type made?

_____

_____

_____

_____

_____

_____

_____

_____

_____

_____

_____

_____

_____

_____

_____

ROCKS AND MINERALS can be found in all kinds of materials. What are some items in your home that you didn't realize were made from rocks or minerals? What are some items that you did realize were made from rocks or minerals?

PAINT CAN BE MADE from powdered rocks and minerals. Can you name any rocks or minerals that are used for making paints? Which rocks or minerals in your area do you think would make good paint pigments?

FOSSILS ARE THE REMNANTS of plants and animals from long ago that were trapped in the earth. Why do you think it's important that scientists study fossils?

WOULD YOU LIKE to be an archaeologist and go on digs to explore and discover fossils? Why or why not?

_____

_____

_____

_____

_____

_____

_____

_____

_____

_____

_____

_____

_____

_____

_____

_____

LANDFORMS, SUCH AS HILLS, MOUNTAINS, AND VALLEYS,

are key features of our landscapes. Look around where you live. Can you describe the landforms that appear in your landscape?

AS MOUNTAIN RANGES AGE, their peaks start to round down and the mountains become smaller. This happens over millions of years. When you compare the Rocky Mountains with the Appalachian Mountains, which do you think is the older mountain range? Why?

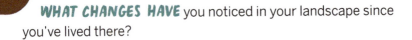

WHAT CHANGES HAVE you noticed in your landscape since you've lived there?

ARE YOU DRAWN to a particular landscape? If you live on the plains, perhaps you wish you could see the mountains occasionally. Or maybe you live in the mountains and like how the desert looks, complete with sand and cacti.

OBSERVATIONS:

_____

_____

_____

QUESTIONS:

_____

_____

NOTES AND SKETCHES:

OBSERVATIONS:

QUESTIONS:

NOTES AND SKETCHES:

Sea

Gulf

Bay

Strait

Confluence

Isthmus

River

Cove

Stream

Delta

Lake

Fjord

Cape

Inlet

Sound

Channel

Peninsula

Ocean

THE WATER THAT SURROUNDS US

3

It's time to dive into the water that covers Earth! Water is all around us in many shapes and forms. From rivers and lakes to oceans and seas, water not only shapes the land we live on, but it also provides a multitude of habitats for many living creatures and plants. In this section, you'll be exploring the different types of water and their ecosystems.

CAN YOU THINK of ways water is important to us and our Earth?

DO YOU NOTICE the bodies of water all around you? From mud puddles in your neighborhood to the river you might cross over to get to the next town, bodies of water are everywhere. What types of bodies of water have you seen in your community?

HOW ARE THE BODIES of water in your area important to your community?

THINK ABOUT THE SOURCES of the bodies of water in your area (for example, rainfall that creates puddles or a river that feeds into a local lake). What would happen if the water source was removed for one of the bodies of water in your community?

BODIES OF WATER also create natural borders for landscapes. They frame continents, countries, states, and even cities with their edges. Think about the body of water closest to your home. Does it create a natural border?

WHAT HAPPENS TO SALT when it is stirred into a glass of fresh water?

SALT WATER IS DENSER than fresh water. That's why it is easier to float in salt water than in fresh water. Why do you think salt water is denser than fresh water?

FRESH WATER FREEZES at 32 degrees Fahrenheit, while salt water freezes at 28.4 degrees Fahrenheit. Why do you think it takes colder temperatures to freeze salt water?

BRACKISH WATER IS FOUND where fresh water meets salt water, such as the point where a river flows into an ocean. Can you think of any other places where brackish water might occur? Do you think brackish water is more or less dense than fresh water?

THERE ARE MANY TYPES of freshwater ecosystems, including ponds, creeks, lakes, and rivers. Is there a freshwater ecosystem near you? What can you observe there?

THREE GROUPS of living organisms are found in a freshwater ecosystem: producers, consumers, and decomposers. What is the purpose of each? What would happen if one or more groups were removed from the ecosystem?

AMONG THE SPECIES that live in freshwater ecosystems are many types of fish, water bugs, and frogs. What is your favorite fresh-water creature and why?

rly Stage Tadpoles

Eggs

Late Stage Tadpoles

Adult Frog

MARINE CREATURES LIVE in saltwater ecosystems such as the ocean. What is your favorite marine creature and why?

THREE MAIN ZONES are located in a marine ecosystem: the splash zone, the intertidal zone, and the low-tide zone. Which is your favorite zone, and what creatures live in it?

OBSERVATIONS:

_____

_____

_____

QUESTIONS:

_____

_____

NOTES AND SKETCHES:

OBSERVATIONS:

QUESTIONS:

NOTES AND SKETCHES:

The Anatomy of a TREE

Top

Branches

Foliage

Crown

Limb

Branch

Twig

Trunk

Shallow Root

Tap Root

Root Hairs

THE PLANTS IN BETWEEN

Whether you look up or down, plants most likely grow all around you. In this section, you will explore trees, bushes, and plants. Whether you live in an arid location, a tropical location, or a plains location, plants play an important role in your natural world.

4

GO OUTSIDE AND LOOK AROUND at the plants that grow in your neighborhood. What do you see? When you look up, do you see the tops of trees? At eye level, are there a variety of bushes? What grows down around your feet?

WHAT KINDS OF TREES grow in your backyard or neighborhood? Are there different types of trees, or are they all the same?

SOME TREES, SUCH AS EVERGREENS, are secure homes for both seasonal and year-round creatures, whereas deciduous trees are better suited for summertime homes. Which kind of habitat do the trees in your backyard or neighborhood offer to the wildlife in your area?

WHAT KINDS OF ANIMALS do you think live (or have you seen living) in the trees?

TREES CAN PROVIDE US with many resources. How many items can you think of that come from trees?

BUSHES ALSO PROVIDE humans and animals with many resources. How are bushes helpful for animals? What do they provide humans with?

VIBRANT WILDFLOWERS ARE PRETTY to look at and good at attracting insects. Why do you think some flowers attract specific insects while others seem to attract all kinds of insects?

SOME FLOWERS RELY on insects and birds for pollination. Bees, butterflies, and moths are types of pollinators. Can you think of others? Have you ever observed an insect or bird pollinating a flower?

SOME PLANTS, SUCH AS RAGWEED, do not have showy flowers. Why do you think that is? What makes them different from plants with showy, colorful flowers?

MUSHROOMS ARE NOT PLANTS; they come from the fungi king-dom. Can you name some ways that mushrooms are different from plants? What do you think their purpose is?

OBSERVATIONS:

_____

_____

_____

QUESTIONS:

_____

_____

NOTES AND SKETCHES:

OBSERVATIONS:

QUESTIONS:

NOTES AND SKETCHES:

THE CREATURES IN BETWEEN

If you're curious about birds, animals, or insects, this is the section for you! You'll have a chance to observe many kinds of critters that roam Earth. From the birds that fill the sky to the furry animals that may pass through your own backyard to the smallest of insects that crawl and fly, the natural world is full of fascinating creatures!

5

DIFFERENT KINDS OF BIRDS live in different locations. For instance, in a city, you would probably observe a lot of pigeons and sparrows, whereas in a more suburban setting, you would probably see a variety of songbirds. What kinds of birds live in your neighborhood?

CAN YOU TELL if the bird you are looking at is male or female? A good rule of thumb is that male birds are often more colorful than female birds. Why do you think this is true?

HAVE YOU EVER SPENT the afternoon watching birds? Do you see birds most often in pairs or in random groups? Or both? Do the bird groups change depending on the type of bird you're watching?

SCIENTISTS ESTIMATE THAT BETWEEN 2 million and 30 million types of insects are crawling, buzzing, and flying on Earth. What insects can be found in your neighborhood? Try to list at least 10 insects!

INSECTS ARE BENEFICIAL, even if you think they're just pests. Can you think of any benefits that insects offer?

ANTS CAN CARRY objects 50 times their own weight with their jaws! What would you do if you could lift objects that weighed 50 times as much as you?

SPIDERS ARE NOT INSECTS; they're actually arachnids! Look at the shape of a spider and the shape of an insect, like an ant. How does the spider look different from the insect? What other differences do you observe?

BUTTERFLIES AND MOTHS are unique insects because they start out as caterpillars. What types of butterflies and moths do you have in your area? What do their caterpillars look like?

PAY ATTENTION TO THE ANIMALS that you see in your back-yard, neighborhood, and larger community. What kinds of animals do you see regularly? Are you seeing the same animals every day or different animals?

OF THE ANIMALS you've observed in your neighborhood, which one is your favorite? What have you noticed while observing that animal?

WHEN YOU SEE ANIMALS in your backyard or neighborhood, are they looking for food? If so, what kind of food do they eat?

NOCTURNAL ANIMALS SLEEP through the day and are active at night. Have you ever seen a nocturnal animal out during the day? If so, what kind of animal was it, and what kind of food do you think it was looking for?

OUR DOMESTIC DOGS AND CATS have descended from wild animals. What wild animals are they related to? Would these wild animals make good pets, too? Why or why not?

OBSERVATIONS:

_____

_____

QUESTIONS:

_____

_____

NOTES AND SKETCHES:

OBSERVATIONS:

_____

_____

_____

QUESTIONS:

_____

_____

NOTES AND SKETCHES:

QUESTIONS:

NOTES AND SKETCHES:

ABOUT THE AUTHOR

Kristine Brown, RH (AHG), is an herbalist and homeschooling mother of six children. She is the writer and illustrator of the online children's publication *Herbal Roots* zine and the creator of several online courses that teach children about botany, drawing, and herbs. She is also the author of three books: *Herbalism at Home: 125 Recipes for Everyday Health*; *The Homesteader's Guide to Growing Herbs: Learn to Grow, Prepare, and Use Herbs*; and *Nature Anatomy Activities for Kids: Fun, Hands-On Learning*. Kristine lives on a homestead with her partner, their two youngest children, and a variety of cats, dogs, chickens, and goats.

CPSIA information can be obtained
at www.ICGtesting.com
Printed in the USA
BVHW091429200522
637646BV00022B/758

9 781685 392703